The Greatest Prophet

Second Edition Large Print

Who was the Greatest Prophet? Can we prove it? What do the scriptures reveal?

Pieter C Voges

The Greatest Prophet

Disclaimer

This eBook is designed to provide information and motivation to our readers. It may contain links to other websites or content belonging to or originating from third parties or links to websites and features. Such external links are not investigated, monitored, or checked for accuracy, adequacy, validity, reliability, availability or completeness.

All information in this eBooks is provided in good faith, however we make no representation or warranty of any kind, express or implied, regarding the accuracy, adequacy, validity, reliability, availability, or completeness of any information.

Photos are provided to assist in comprehension, but are not from actual events. They are from royalty free stock photos.

The Greatest Prophet

Contents

The Greatest Prophet

Introduction

Most people are aware of Jesus Christ as our Savior. Few understand Him as the Greatest Prophet.

Throughout history some have claimed to be prophets sent by God. We need to consider this topic with all seriousness and reverence. We need to search the scriptures to understand the Will of God.

Israel of old was warned by God not to accept just any prophet, as they may be false prophets:

"And Jehovah said to me, The prophets prophesy lies in My name; I did not send them, nor have I commanded them, nor did I speak to them. They prophesy to you a false vision and a worthless divination, and a thing of no value, and the deceit of their heart."
(Jeremiah 14:14, MKJV)

At His first advent, Jesus also personally warned His followers about following false prophets. They will appear godly and religious, yet mislead unsuspecting people.

"Beware of false prophets who come to you in sheep's clothing, but inwardly they are ravening wolves.
You shall know them by their fruits. Do men gather grapes from thorns, or figs from thistles?
(Matthew 7:15-16, MKJV)

Jesus warned people to be very careful. People must look at the results of following the prophet. Does it bring peace?

The Apostle Peter also warned the people. He highlighted one aspect of measurement:

"But there were also false prophets among the people, even as there will be false teachers among you, who secretly will bring in destructive heresies, even denying the Master who bought them, bringing on themselves swift destruction."
(1 Peter 2:1, MKJV)

In one of the last books of the Bible, the Apostle John gave us a more precise indication:

"Beloved, do not believe every spirit, but try the spirits to see if they are of God, because many false prophets have gone out into the world.
By this you know the Spirit of God: every spirit that confesses that Jesus Christ has come in the flesh is of God;
and every spirit that does not confess that Jesus Christ has come in the flesh is not of God. And this is the antichrist you heard is coming, and even now is already in the world"
(1 John 4:1-3, MKJV)

It is essential to understand and accept that Jesus Christ pre-existed as the Son of God. He came in the flesh to be subject to death at the hands of mankind. This way we can understand just how bad humankind in general is.

Serious followers need to study more and make sure about whom they are following.

The Greatest Prophet

Chapter 1

Definition of a Prophet

What is a prophet? How can one define a prophet? What is an example of a prophet?

Direct communication

The universally accepted prophet of the Old Testament was Moses. Let's notice Moses as an example and definition of a prophet of God. God called Moses, and he responded positively with total dedication and unwavering faith.

Notice what God said to him. Notice how God said he must announce his status and relationship, which defined him:

"And Moses said to God, Behold, when I come to the sons of Israel, and shall say to them, The God of your fathers has sent me to you, and they shall say to me, What is His name? What shall I say to them?
And God said to Moses, I AM THAT I AM. And He said, So you shall say to the sons of Israel, I AM has sent me to you.

And God said to Moses again, You shall say this to the sons of Israel, Jehovah the God of your fathers, the God of Abraham, the God of Isaac, and the God of Jacob, has sent me to you. This is My name forever, and this is My title from generation to generation."
(Exodus 3:13-15, MKJV)

Notice how God identifies Himself through Moses. He identifies Himself as the God of Abraham, Isaac, and Jacob. This is what the scriptures defined. And further, He defined Moses as the one who received direct instructions from God. The heavenly Father communicated directly with the human, Moses. This direct relationship was highlighted several times throughout the scriptures. And a prophet would only relate to people that which he was told to say - nothing more, nothing less.

God the Father also talked directly with Abraham:

"And Jehovah said to Abram, Go out of your country, and from your kindred, and from your father's house into a land that I will show you.
And I will make you a great nation. And I will bless you and make your name great. And you shall be a blessing. And I will bless those that bless you and curse the one who curses you. And in you shall all families of the earth be blessed.
And Abram departed, even as Jehovah had spoken to him. And Lot went with him. And Abram was seventy-five years old when he departed from Haran."
(Genesis 12:1-4, MKJV)

God also directly talked Samuel:

"And Jehovah came and stood, and called as at other times, Samuel, Samuel! Then Samuel answered, Speak, for Your servant hears."
(1 Samuel 3:10, MKJV)

God also directly talked to Elijah:

"And he came there to a cave and stayed there. And behold, the Word of Jehovah came to him, and He said to him, What are you doing here, Elijah?"
(1 Kings 19:9, MKJV)

This was also the case with Ezekiel:

"Coming the Word of Jehovah became known to Ezekiel, the son of Buzi, the priest in the land of the Chaldeans by the river Chebar. And the hand of Jehovah was on him there."
(Ezekiel 1:3, MKJV)

And as usual, also with Jeremiah:

"And it happened, the Word of Jehovah came to me, saying,"
(Jeremiah 1:4, MKJV)

We can see that God Almighty spoke directly with the prophets. These prophets were worshipping God and walking faithfully and truthfully before God, unwavering in their dedication. They were spiritually close enough to God to have a direct conversation with God. We don't find intermediate agents involved. Sometimes – after the initial contact – further communications may happen through angels. However, there was always this direct contact through the presence of God, talking through the power of His Spirit.

No radical new revelation

Furthermore, the revelation from God is progressive, and builds as human history continues. This makes sense as it is the same God that is busy with His plan of salvation for mankind. Since mankind turned its back on God in the Garden of Eden, mankind is playing to the wiles of Satan the devil, and is going from war to war. But God has a long term plan, and will intervene at certain stages. He will be ready when mankind will face annihilation and will desperately seek the Messiah. Even though they have drifted so far away, Messiah will respond even if they will hardly recognize Him when He returns. However it all works to that inevitable point in human history. Hence it is always the same God that is working towards the same goal. Some individuals will repent and seek His ways and laws, and will worship Him, leading to obedience.

So a prophet will not come with a radical new plan. It will always happen according to predefined guidance.

This way the people can always discern between false prophets and a real prophet sent by God:

"And when they shall say to you, Seek to the mediums and to wizards who peep and mutter; should not a people seek to their God, than for the living to the dead?
To the Law and to the testimony! If they do not speak according to this Word, it is because no light is in them." (Isaiah 8:19-20, MKJV)

A true prophet of God will obey God's Law contained in Commandments and covenants, and his message will be inside the confines of the overall testimony of God's plan of salvation.

If an apparent prophet comes and declares a message that is not in line with what has been defined by the prophets of the Old Testament scriptures that was promulgated by the God of Abraham, Isaac and Jacob, one has to question his calling from the outset. Many questions must be asked. Many conditions must be fulfilled. If the prophet fails these, then walk away!

Jesus as prophet

To some extent, one may question Jesus's assertion that He was a prophet, for He seems to have changed the worship. According to some general Christian leaders, He changed a lot of things! Can that be acceptable? Jesus must have followed predetermined scriptures, or He can be seen as false.

For instance, the notion of many is that Jesus changed the day of worship from the Saturday Sabbath of the 4th Commandment to Sunday. However, there are Christians that still keep the Sabbath according to the 4th Commandment.

Was Jesus a true prophet of God?

We need to investigate this in greater detail. We will measure Jesus Christ. And then others that claim to be prophets must also be subjected to the same scrutiny.

What did Moses, the first major prophet, say about Jesus?

Before the nation Israel entered the Promised Land, Moses gave them a warning:

"For these nations whom you shall possess listened to
observers of clouds and to diviners. But as for you,
Jehovah your God has not allowed you to do so.
Jehovah your God will raise up to you a Prophet from
the midst of you, of your brothers, One like me. To Him
you shall listen,"
(Deuteronomy 18:14-15, MKJV)

Moses said that while Israel was in the Promised Land, another prophet will be raised to the stature of Moses. The people of Israel must listen to Him and follow Him.

He will live and preach in Judea and is expected to cause a revival in and around Jerusalem.

It is true that other prophets came like Elijah and Jeremiah, but they were sent to steady the course of Israel, and to be sure that Israel would occupy Judea when Messiah came, even if it took a restoration of Israel initiated by Daniel and fulfilled by Ezra and Nehemiah. This would be as one of the final prophets of the Old Testament era indicated:

"Behold, I will send My messenger, and He will clear the way before Me. And Jehovah, whom you seek, shall suddenly come to His temple, even the Angel of the Covenant, in whom you delight. Behold, He comes, says Jehovah of Hosts."
(Malachi 3:1, MKJV)

So the great prophet that Moses prophesied would come, would make his appearance in Judea, and would come to the Temple in Jerusalem. Another prophet would prepare the way for Him by educating disciples. Then they could be used by the ultimate greatest prophet of all time. His timing would be according to the Creator's Time Matrix, on time, and according to God's purposes.

John the Baptist, in the spirit of Elijah

Another prophet would prepare the way before the Messiah:

"Remember the Law of Moses My servant, which I commanded to him in Horeb for all Israel, the statutes and judgments.
Behold, I am sending you Elijah the prophet before the coming of the great and dreadful day of Jehovah.
And he shall turn the heart of the fathers to the sons, and the heart of the sons to their fathers, that I not come and strike the earth with utter destruction.
(Malachi 4:4-5, MKJV)

The one that prepared the way before the First Advent of Jesus Christ was John the Baptist. Jesus discussed this with His disciples:

"And as they departed, Jesus began to say to the crowds concerning John, What did you go out into the wilderness to see? A reed shaken with the wind?
But what did you go out to see? A man clothed in soft clothing? Behold, they who wear soft clothing are in kings' houses.
But what did you go out to see? A prophet? Yea, I say to you, and one more excellent than a prophet.

For this is the one of whom it is written, "Behold, I send My messenger before Your face, who shall prepare Your way before You."
Truly I say to you, Among those who have been born of women there has not risen a greater one than John the Baptist. But the least in the kingdom of Heaven is greater than he."
(Matthew 11:7-11, MKJV)

John the Baptist came to prepare the way. Jesus viewed him as the greatest up to that point. But since Jesus was from the kingdom of Heaven, He was obviously greater. This was the implication of what He said. If not, then John was the greatest, and hence the one that Moses talked about. However, that will diminish Jesus, which obviously is not the case! No, Jesus showed that even though John the Baptist suffered much reproach and even jail time, he stayed the course and was completely truthful, making him the greatest prophet up to that point. However, as a member of the kingdom of Heaven, Jesus was greater, making Him the greatest Prophet of all time.

Any person or prophet that denies the pre-existence of Jesus as a member of the kingdom of Heaven is not from God, according to the scriptures.

John the Baptist came and fulfilled the Elijah mission, preparing the way for Jesus the Christ by educating and preparing some people to become disciples of Jesus. Hence he was alive when Jesus began His ministry, to hand over educated and converted disciples.

This will be the same before Christ's second coming.

"And His disciples asked Him, saying, Why then do the scribes say that Elijah must come first?
And answering Jesus said to them, Elijah truly shall come first and restore all things.
But I say to you that Elijah has come already, and they did not know him, but have done to him whatever they desired. Likewise also the Son of Man shall suffer from them.
Then His disciples understood that He spoke to them about John the Baptist."
(Matthew 17:10-13, MKJV)

John the Baptist was a great prophet that came in the mold and purpose of Elijah. His ministry started before Christ's ministry but overlapped. Christ's first advent was a continuation and expansion of what John the Baptist started.

But another prophet will come just before Christ's Second Advent. He will also prepare the way before Christ. He will raise a following that will be ready to follow Christ when He comes. This second incident of an Elijah type prophet will be alive when Christ comes.

John the Baptist was very humble initially and would not take on the cloak of Elijah until Christ was manifested and began His ministry in power and wonders. Only once Christ was manifested would John the Baptist admit to having been that initial prophet.

"And this is the witness of John, when the Jews sent priests and Levites from Jerusalem to ask him, Who are you?
And he confessed and did not deny, but confessed, I am not the Christ.
And they asked him, What then? Are you Elijah? And he says, I am not. Are you that prophet? And he answered, No.
Then they said to him, Who are you so that we may give an answer to those who sent us? What do you say of yourself?
He said, I am "the voice of one crying in the wilderness: Make straight the way of the Lord," as the prophet Isaiah said.
And they who were sent were from the Pharisees.
And they asked him and said, Why then do you baptize, if you are not the Christ, nor Elijah, nor that Prophet?
John answered them, saying, I baptize with water, but One stands among you whom you do not know.
He it is who, coming after me, who has been before me; of whom I am not worthy to loosen the thong of His sandal."
(John 1:19-27, MKJV)

So we know that the next significant prophet that will lead the way before Christ will be busy doing his ministry when Christ returns. We also know that he will not be keen to be clothed with the cloak of Elijah until Christ returns. He will definitely not go out and declare himself as the great prophet. Any person that wanted to declare himself as that great prophet since Christ's first advent, and have died long ago, cannot be that prophet.

Prophets after Christ?

Would there be more prophets after Christ? Would there be more prophets till Christ Second Advent? What did the Church understand?

The apostle Paul explained:

"And God set some in the church, firstly, apostles; secondly, prophets; thirdly, teachers, then works of power, then gifts of healings, helps, governments, kinds of languages.
Are all apostles? Are all prophets? Are all teachers? Are all workers of power?
Do all have gifts of healings? Do all speak languages? Do all interpret?
But zealously strive after the better gifts. And yet I show to you a more excellent way."
(1 Corinthians 12:28-31, MKJV)

We see that it was accepted that some would continue to be prophets. However, in what way would they be prophets?

Notice that apostles were considered greater than prophets! How can that be? Was the apostle Paul greater than Christ! What did Paul mean?

Lest continue:

"And if there are two or three prophets, let them speak, and let the others judge."
(1 Corinthians 14:29, MKJV)

Why would others have to judge?

The issue is that nobody can speak anything that is outside the Law, the covenants, and the overall testimony. Hence prophets that came after Christ and the Apostles need to be judged. But the issue goes further.

Paul describes that prophets are people with a gift of understanding and explaining what the prophets of old meant. They can read from Old Testament scriptures and correctly explain the meanings. But it can only happen in a setting where others can listen and judge if the layout is according to the previously understood overall testimony, and does not violate any of God's Law. This is implied in the following verse:

"And the spirits of the prophets are subject to the prophets."
(1 Corinthian 14:32, MKJV)

So those that want to prophesy can only do so by referring to the scriptures of ancient prophets. They cannot begin a completely new story. They are subject to the ancient prophecies, and can only explain and highlight. No radical new prophecy is acceptable, as the follow on verse explains:

"For God is not the author of confusion, but of peace, as in all churches of the saints."
(1 Corinthians 14:33, MKJV)

There cannot be confusion and conflict with prior prophecies. God is the same forever. God obviously will not be in conflict with Himself.

Any person that claims to be a prophet in the mold of Elijah must be suspect, for the coming prophet will not claim to be the one unless Christ is manifested in his lifetime at the Second Advent. And he cannot disagree with the Law and prophets of old. Such a person must be rejected.

"If anyone thinks to be a prophet, or a spiritual one, let him recognize the things I write to you, that they are a commandment of the Lord."
(1 Corinthians 14:37, MKJV)

Any person that claims to be a prophet but denies Jesus as the Christ, as explained by Paul and the twelve Apostles, must be rejected.

The Greatest Prophet

Chapter 2

Prophecies of Jesus the Christ

Did Jesus prophesy? Did He foretell what would happen? And did it happen as He predicted? This is one of the signs of a great prophet.

"And if you say in your heart, How shall we know the word which Jehovah has not spoken?
When a prophet speaks in the name of Jehovah, if the thing does not follow nor come to pass, that is the thing which Jehovah has not spoken. The prophet has spoken it presumptuously. You shall not be afraid of him."
(Deuteronomy 18:21-22, MKJV)

A great prophet must at least have prophesied some future events. He will then be tested by whether those events do happen as he prophesied. If a "prophet" never prophesied events that he can be tested against, he is not a great prophet.

We will look at some of Jesus' prophecies.

Prophesied His betrayal

"And as they ate, He said, Truly I say to you that one of
you will betray Me."
(Matthew 26:21, MKJV)

Did this happen? We all know the story:

"And as He was yet speaking, behold, Judas came, one
of the Twelve. And with him came a great crowd with
swords and clubs, being sent from the chief priests and
elders of the people.
And he who betrayed Him gave them a sign, saying,
Whomever I shall kiss, He is the one, lay hold on Him.
And coming up to Jesus immediately, he said, Hail,
Master! And he kissed Him."
(Matthew 26:47-49, MKJV)

Judas did betray Jesus as He prophesied.

Peter's denial

What about Peter? Jesus also prophesied about the
apostle Peter:

"Peter answered and said to Him, though all shall be
offended because of You, I will never be offended.
Jesus said to him, Truly I say to you that this night,
before the cock crows, you shall deny Me three times."
(Matthew 26:33-34, MKJV)

Did this happen?

"And Peter sat outside in the court. And a girl came to him, saying, You also were with Jesus of Galilee.
But he denied all before them, saying, I do not know what you say.
And when he had gone out into the porch, another saw him and said to those there, This one was also with Jesus of Nazareth.
And again he denied with an oath, I do not know the man.
And after a little while those who stood by came and said to Peter, Surely you also are one of them, for your speech betrays you.
Then he began to curse and to swear, I do not know the man. And immediately the cock crowed.
And Peter remembered the word of Jesus, Who said to him, Before the cock crows, you shall deny Me three times. And he went out and wept bitterly."
(Matthew 26:69-75, MKJV)

It happened exactly as Jesus prophesied!

The fall and destruction of cities

Did Jesus predict more significant events, such as the destruction of cities? After Jesus preached in some cities and nobody in those cities repented and came to Him, He predicted their eternal destruction!

"Then He began to upbraid the cities in which most of
His mighty works were done, because they did not
repent.
Woe to you, Chorazin! Woe to you, Bethsaida! For if the
powerful acts which were done in you had been done in
Tyre and Sidon, they would have repented long ago in
sackcloth and ashes!
But I say to you, It shall be more tolerable for Tyre and
Sidon in the day of judgment than for you.
And you, Capernaum, who are exalted to the heaven,
shall be brought down to hell. For if the mighty works
which have been done in you had been done in Sodom, it
would have remained until this day.
But I say to you, it shall be more tolerable for the land of
Sodom in the day of judgment than for you."
(Matthew 11:20 – 24, MKJV)

These cities were eventually destroyed by the Romans.
They were never rebuilt to their former glory. Other
cities like Jerusalem, Bethlehem, and Hebron, however,
remained to this day. Jesus' prophecies were fulfilled!

Destruction of the Temple

One of the most incredible prophecies of Jesus was the destruction of the physical Temple in Jerusalem:

"And Jesus went out and departed from the temple. And His disciples came to Him to show Him the buildings of the temple.
And Jesus said to them, Do you not see all these things? Truly I say to you, There shall not be left here one stone on another that shall not be thrown down."
(Matthew 24:1-2, MKJV)

This happened in about the year 70AD as prophesied. This remarkable fulfillment is discussed in another eBook called "The Sign of Jonah – expanded". The Temple was never rebuilt. To this day, all that remained was the foundation floor and the Wailing Wall. For Christianity to spread the physical Temple was no longer required. The sacrificial law was fulfilled in Christ's sufferings, and forever no animal sacrifices would ever be made for the forgiveness of sin. Any people or church that would do them does not understand Christianity at all. It would be an affront to God if it continued.

Christianity would spread worldwide

Jesus prophesied that Christianity would flourish and spread worldwide:

"And I also say to you that you are Peter, and on this rock I will build My church, and the gates of hell shall not prevail against it.
And I will give the keys of the kingdom of Heaven to you. And whatever you may bind on earth shall occur, having been bound in Heaven, and whatever you may loose on earth shall occur, having been loosed in Heaven."
(Matthew 16:18-19, MKJV)

Christianity would spread, and nothing can stop it, even if the apostles and disciples were killed by governments at the behest of false religions. It was decided in Heaven long ago, and it is happening! This did happen, as is evident by all people worldwide.

False prophets

One remarkable prophecy of Jesus Christ can be found in the book of Matthew, in chapter 24. We will do well to have a look at some of the verses.

"And as He sat on the Mount of Olives, the disciples came to Him privately, saying, Tell us, when shall these things be? And what shall be the sign of Your coming, and of the end of the world?
And Jesus answered and said to them, Take heed that no man deceive you.
For many will come in My name, saying, I am Christ, and will deceive many."
(Matthew 24:3-5, MKJV)

Jesus predicted that there would be many false people that would want to say that they are the returned Christ. This happened in the first century in and around Jerusalem. There is also the connotation that some false preachers would come and acknowledge that Jesus was the Christ, but would twist His words and deceive many. This has happened.

"And you will hear of wars and rumors of wars. See that you are not troubled, for all these things must occur; but the end is not yet.
For nation will rise against nation, and kingdom against kingdom. And there will be famines and pestilences and earthquakes in different places.

All these are the beginning of sorrows."
(Matthew 24:6-8, MKJV)

This has happened and is happening today as we are nearing the End Time. Just watch the news channels!

"Then they will deliver you up to be afflicted and will kill you. And you will be hated of all nations for My name's sake.
And then many will be offended, and will betray one another, and will hate one another."
(Matthew 24:9-10, MKJV)

We see more and more killings and beheadings in the name of God when the truth is that God is absolutely pro-life. And there have been reports of peaceful Christians being killed by radicals of other religions as predicted.

"And many false prophets will rise and deceive many.
And because iniquity shall abound, the love of many will become cold."
(Matthew 24:11-12, MKJV)

False prophets did come! Even in the name of Christ! Then they teach people to work iniquity (breaking the Ten Commandments and causing confusion).

"But he who endures to the end, the same shall be kept safe.

And this gospel of the kingdom shall be proclaimed in all the world as a witness to all nations. And then the end shall come."
(Matthew 24:13-14, MKJV)

We must be willing to stand up for Jesus Christ, or we will perish. The Gospel is still going out in many ways to the ends of the world today.

"Therefore when you see the abomination of desolation, spoken of by Daniel the prophet, stand in the holy place (whoever reads, let him understand)."
(Matthew 24:15, MKJV)

The "abomination of desolation" refers to war machines. But it is precipitated by other actions, such as unholy things being brought in to the Temple mount. In about 70AD, it was reported that Roman officers wanted to bring a pig into the Temple to be sacrificed for the Romans, which led to a revolt by the Jews, which in turn caused the Romans to bring in their war machines, causing fulfillment of this prophecy.

"Then let those in Judea flee into the mountains.
Let him on the housetop not come down to take anything out of his house;
nor let him in the field turn back to take his clothes.
And woe to those who are with child, and to those who give suck in those days!"
Matthew 24:16-18, MKJV)

The disciples did heed this warning. When the Romans came with their war machines to destroy the Temple, the disciples fled south to a city called Petra. Those that heeded the prophecy were saved.

We sometimes find duality in prophecy. Just as John the Baptist came to teach others and introduce them to Christ, so a future prophet in the mold of Elijah will come just before the return of Christ. In the same fashion, prophecies given by Jesus here, will also spill over to the End Time, and will play out in the Last Days. People in Jerusalem will again have to flee when the world armies arrive for the final conflict.

"But pray that your flight is not in the winter, nor on the sabbath day;
for then shall be great tribulation, such as has not been since the beginning of the world to this time; no, nor ever shall be.
And unless those days should be shortened, no flesh would be saved. But for the elect's sake, those days shall be shortened."
Matthew 24:20-22, MKJV)

When nuclear missiles begin to fly, we will reach the possibility that life can be eradicated from the earth. The nuclear winter will come due to radioactive debris clouds circling the earth. This will lead to crop failures and hunger. It can also distort the genes of future people and animals. Most life can fail to reproduce. Most flesh can indeed die out. But Christ will return to stop the madness. There are prophecies that must be fulfilled.

The saints must be resurrected and receive their reward as leaders of a future generation on the earth for a millennium. Some life must be saved for the plan of mankind's salvation to continue. So the terrible days of the End Time will be shortened. Humanity will not have lived out the six millenniums allowed as per Adam and Eve's rebellion, and all humanity since then. Ever since the new humanoids received a spirit to understand the communication from God about six millenniums ago and disobeyed, the allotted six days of millenniums were allowed where humanity continues without God's reign till humanity self-destructs. But God loves us and is still intervening to save humankind.

"Then if any man shall say to you, Lo, here is Christ! Or, There! Do not believe it.
For false Christs and false prophets will arise and show great signs and wonders; so much so that, if it were possible, they would deceive even the elect.
Behold, I have told you beforehand."
(Matthew 24:23-25, MKJV)

Jesus knew that false prophets and religious leaders would come. And look at the world today. It is still the case after all these years.

"Therefore if they shall say to you, Behold, He is in the desert! Do not go out. Behold, He is in the secret rooms! Do not believe it.
For as the lightning comes out of the east and shines even to the west, so also will be the coming of the Son of Man.

For wherever the carcass is, there the eagles will be gathered.
(Matthew 24:26-28, MKJV)

Jesus indicated that His return would be from Heaven, and He will be seen above as the clouds. It will be supernatural, and there will be no mistake about who He is. From above Jerusalem, He will be seen from all Judea. One can just imagine how news media and the Internet will stream the event to the ends of the earth. True Christians will be gathered to the One that the people slaughtered at the crucifixion. Like eagles, they will gather to worship the One that sacrificed Himself for their sake!

"And immediately after the tribulation of those days, the sun shall be darkened and the moon shall not give her light, and the stars shall fall from the heaven, and the powers of the heavens shall be shaken."
(Matthew 24:29, MKJV)

NASA and other space agencies are becoming more and more aware of the dangers of rogue meteors and asteroids that may suddenly arrive at the earth. If they strike the earth in various places, the dust may circle the earth and blot out the great lights in the sky. Humanity will certainly know when Christ returns.

What a Great Prophet was Jesus Christ! Have some of these things not happened? Has the world not developed to the point where nations are poised to strike at each other? Have the war machines not developed to the point where life on earth can be wiped out? Have the Internet and news media not developed where the world can watch when an earthshattering even happen?

We have only scratched the surface and discussed a fraction of what He prophesied, but it is certainly enough to prove that He was a Great Prophet!

Chapter 3

The Qualifications of Christ

Was Jesus just a prophet? Does He also have other roles in the Kingdom of God? Does He also have other titles of office?

The Glory of God

Jesus is considered the glory of God:

"looking for the blessed hope, and the appearance of the glory of our great God and Savior Jesus Christ,"
(Titus 2:13, MKJV)

Jesus glorifies God. God adore Jesus Christ.

"And Jesus, when He had been baptized, went up immediately out of the water. And lo, the heavens were opened to Him, and He saw the Spirit of God descending like a dove and lighting upon Him.
And lo, a voice from Heaven, saying, This is My beloved Son, in whom I am well pleased."
(Matthew 3:16-17, MKJV)

Jesus carries the most favor with God compared to any other angel, elder, prophet, or anybody in the service of God.

Our Co-creator

Jesus was instrumental in our creation:

"For all things were created in Him, the things in the heavens, and the things on the earth, the visible and the invisible, whether thrones or dominions or principalities or powers, all things were created through Him and for Him."
(Colossians 1:16, MKJV)

Jesus was the only begotten Son of God. Through His guidance and influence, and His power over the angels, the universe was created.

"In the beginning was the Word, and the Word was with God, and the Word was God.
He was in the beginning with God.
All things came into being through Him, and without Him not even one thing came into being that has come into being."
(John 1:1-3, MKJV)

We exist because Jesus Christ worked for and with God for us to be.

Satan may have stolen us in the Garden of Eden, and humankind was foolish enough to believe him, but the One that was instrumental in our existence is still working to save us from deception and to gather us to salvation and eternal life.

Our Lord

We are to accept Jesus as Lord in our lives. He has power over the saints.

"And Jesus came and spoke to them, saying, All authority is given to Me in Heaven and in earth."
(Matthew 28:18, MKJV)

God has granted Him all power and decision making. Jesus will decide in the end if we live or die.

"Truly, truly, I say to you, The hour is coming and now is, when the dead shall hear the voice of the Son of God, and they who hear shall live.
For as the Father has life in Himself, so He has given to the Son to have life within Himself,
and has given Him authority to execute judgment also, because He is the Son of Man."
(John 5:25-27, MKJV)

Jesus holds power over our eternal destiny. It is in His hands!

Our Savior

God wants to save us from eternal death through the saving work of our Savior, His Son, Jesus Christ.

"But when the kindness and love of God our Savior toward man appeared,
not by works of righteousness which we have done, but according to His mercy He saved us, through the washing of regeneration and renewal of the Holy Spirit, whom He poured out on us abundantly through Jesus Christ our Savior,
that being justified by His grace, we should become heirs according to the hope of eternal life."
(Titus 3:4-7, MKJV)

The process of saving us from eternal damnation is bound up in true Christianity. God has sanctioned this process as doable and can lead to eternal life. When it comes to eternal life, there is no other name given, no other process that God will work with.

"This is the Stone which you builders have counted worthless, and He has become the Head of the Corner. And there is salvation in no other One; for there is no other name under Heaven given among men by which we must be saved."
(Acts 4:11-12, MKJV)

Jesus is the only way to eternal salvation. And this Jesus was also the Greatest Prophet ever.

Merciful High Priest

Jesus is also a High Priest for us in Heaven before God.

"where the Forerunner has entered for us, even Jesus, having become a high priest forever after the order of Melchizedek."
(Hebrews 6:20, MKJV)

Originally there was Melchizedek in the city of Salem, which much later became Jerusalem. When the Israelites sinned in the desert during the Exodus, another physical priesthood was implemented with Aaron as the high priest. The high priest would intercede for the sinning nation and would work both ways to get the nation to reduce sin, while on the other hand interceding for the nation before God to secure mercy so that God does not forsake them and leave them to self-destruct.

Then came Jesus, the Son of God, who also lived among humanity, to appreciate our failings and yet prove a sinless life in the flesh.

He lived with us and understood our infirmities, our failings, our fears, and our temptations. Hence He is able to make intercession for us before God's Throne.

"But we see Jesus, who was made a little lower than the angels for the suffering of death, crowned with glory and

honor, that He by the grace of God should taste death for all.
For it became Him, for whom are all things and by whom are all things, in bringing many sons into glory, to perfect the Captain of their salvation through sufferings.
For both He who sanctifies and they who are sanctified are all of One, for which cause He is not ashamed to call them brothers,
saying, "I will declare Your name to My brothers; in the midst of the assembly I will sing praise to You."
And again, "I will put My trust in Him." And again, "Behold Me and the children whom God has given Me."
Since then the children have partaken of flesh and blood, He also Himself likewise partook of the same; that through death He might destroy him who had the power of death (that is, the Devil),
and deliver those who through fear of death were all their lifetime subject to bondage.
For truly He did not take the nature of angels, but He took hold of the seed of Abraham.
Therefore in all things it behoved him to be made like His brothers, that He might be a merciful and faithful high priest in things pertaining to God, to make propitiation for the sins of His people.
For in that He Himself has suffered, having been tempted, He is able to rescue those who are being tempted."
Hebrews 2:9-18, MKJV)

So the same Jesus Christ is also our High Priest before God. Therefor effective prayers are prayed by repentant Christians in the Name of Christ.

"No longer do I call you servants, for the servant does not know what his master does. But I have called you friends, for all things that I have heard from My Father I have made known to you.
You have not chosen Me, but I have chosen you and ordained you that you should go and bring forth fruit, and that your fruit should remain; that whatever you shall ask of the Father in My name, He may give it to you"
(John 15:15-16, MKJV)

So this same Jesus Christ that brought to us incredible prophesies, is also our merciful High Priest, through whom we can receive forgiveness.

Jesus Christ did succeed in everything, and is everything for us, even the Greatest Prophet ever!

Chapter 4

Prophesies fulfilled in Christ

There is an amazing number of prophecies that were fulfilled by Jesus Christ. It would take supernatural ability to do so. This was established so that the world can know for sure that Jesus was not a false prophet. He fulfilled all the prophecies. No other alleged prophet has ever begun to fulfill anything like that. We will look at some of them and list some more for the reader to prove that Jesus Christ was The Great Prophet.

A descendant of Abraham

The Messiah would be a descendant of Abraham, as promised.

"And the Angel of Jehovah called to Abraham out of the heavens the second time,
and said, I have sworn by Myself, says Jehovah; because you have done this thing, and have not withheld your
son, your only one;
that in blessing I will bless you, and in multiplying I will multiply your seed like the stars of the heavens, and as
the sand which is upon the seashore. And your Seed
shall possess the gate of His enemies.

And in your Seed shall all the nations of the earth be blessed, because you have obeyed My voice."
(Genesis 22:15-18, MKJV)

This Seed was Christ.

"And to Abraham and to his Seed the promises were spoken. It does not say, And to seeds, as of many; but as of one, "And to your Seed," which is Christ."
(Galatians 3:16, MKJV)

Matthew showed the genealogy from Abraham to Jesus Christ.

"The book of the genealogy of Jesus Christ, the son of David, the son of Abraham."
(Matthew 1:1, MKJV)

The reader can read the rest of the genealogy in Matthew, chapter 1.

Descendant of Isaac

"And Abraham said to God, Oh that Ishmael might live before You!
And God said, Sarah your wife shall bear you a son indeed. And you shall call his name Isaac. And I will establish My covenant with him for an everlasting covenant, and with his seed after him.
And as for Ishmael, I have heard you. Behold, I have blessed him, and will make him fruitful, and will

multiply him exceedingly. He shall father twelve chiefs, and I will make him a great nation.
But I will establish My covenant with Isaac, whom Sarah shall bear to you at this set time in the next year."
(Genesis 17:18-21, MKJV)

This was the case with Jesus Christ, as can also be seen from Matthew 1:

"Abraham fathered Isaac, and Isaac fathered Jacob, and Jacob fathered Judah and his brothers."
(Matthews 1:2, MKJV)

Descendant of Jacob

This also showed the third prophecy that Jesus would come through the genealogy of Jacob. Notice how Balaam prophesied before Balak concerning Jacob's descendants:

"And Balaam said to Balak, Did I not speak also to your messengers whom you sent to me, saying,
If Balak would give me his house full of silver and gold, I cannot go beyond the mouth of Jehovah, to do good or bad of my own mind. What Jehovah said, that I will speak.
And now, behold, I go to my people. Come! I will make known to you what this people shall do to your people in the latter days.

And he took up his parable, and said, Balaam the son of
Beor has said, and the man whose eyes are open has
said;
he has said, he who heard the words of God and knew
the knowledge of the Most High, who sees the vision of
the Almighty, falling down but having his eyes open;
I shall see him, but not now. I shall behold him, but not
near. There shall come a Star out of Jacob, and a Scepter
shall rise out of Israel, and shall strike the corners of
Moab, and destroy all the sons of tumult."
(Numbers 24:12-17, MKJV)

Jesus was ultimately the Star that came out of Jacob.

From the tribe of Judah

Jacob prophesied in his old age that the genealogy to
Messiah or Shiloh would run through the tribe of Judah.

"The scepter shall not depart from Judah, nor a Lawgiver
from between his feet, until Shiloh come. And the
obedience of the peoples to him."
(Genesis 49:10, MKJV)

Even though God allowed Israel to be taken onto
captivity due to rebellion and disobedience, He still
intervened and allowed Daniel to prophesy and astound
the gentile king, to allow a restoration under Ezra and
Nehemiah. Mainly three tribes returned: the Levites,
Judah (Jews), and Benjamin. It was essential that there
be Jews in Judea from which Messiah could come for the

prophecy to be fulfilled. Hence Jesus was a Jew, fulfilling this prophecy, as can be seen from His conversation with many people during His first advent.

"Then the woman of Samaria said to Him, How do you, being a Jew, ask a drink of me, who am a woman of Samaria? For the Jews do not associate with Samaritans. Jesus answered and said to her, If you knew the gift of God, and who it is that says to you, Give Me to drink, you would have asked of Him, and He would have given you living water."
(John 4:9-10, MKJV)

Born in Bethlehem

"And you, Bethlehem Ephratah, you being least among the thousands of Judah, out of you He shall come forth to Me, to become Ruler in Israel, He whose goings forth have been from of old, from the days of eternity."
(Micah 5:2, MKJV)

And so it was as prophesied:

"And Joseph also went up from Galilee to be taxed (out of the city of Nazareth, into Judea, to the city of David which is called **Bethlehem**, because he was of the house and family line of David).
And he took Mary his betrothed wife, being with child. And while they were there, the days for her deliverance were fulfilled.

And she brought forth her son, the First-born, and wrapped Him, and laid Him in a manger-- because there was no room for them in the inn.
And in the same country there were shepherds living in the field, keeping watch over their flock by night.
And lo, the angel of the Lord came on them, and the glory of the Lord shone around them. And they were grievously afraid.
And the angel said to them, Do not fear. For behold, I give to you good tidings of great joy, which shall be to all people.
For to you is born today, in the city of David, a Savior, who is Christ the Lord."
(Luke 2:4-11, MKJV)

Escaped the slaughter of the children

Jesus would escape the slaughter of the children in Bethlehem, as was foretold:

"So says Jehovah: A voice was heard in Ramah, wailing and bitter weeping; Rachel weeping for her sons; she refuses to be comforted for her sons, because they are not."
(Jeremiah 31:15, MKJV)

And so it happened in Bethlehem:

"Then Herod, when he saw that he was mocked by the wise men, was greatly enraged. And he sent and killed all the boys in Bethlehem, and in all its districts, from two years old and under, according to the time which he had carefully inquired of the wise men.
Then was fulfilled that which was spoken by Jeremiah the prophet, saying,
  "A voice was heard in Ramah, wailing and weeping and great mourning, Rachel weeping for her children, and would not be comforted, because they are not."
(Matthew 2:16-18, MKJV)

Flight to Egypt

After fleeing to Egypt to escape the persecution of Herod, Jesus would eventually be returned to Judea. The favor of God was with Jesus, as it was with Jacob who was renamed Israel:

"When Israel was a child, then I loved him and called My son out of Egypt."
(Hosea 11:1, MKJV)

And this actually happened after Herod died.

"And he was there until the death of Herod; so that it might be fulfilled which was spoken by the LORD through the prophet, "Out of Egypt I have called My Son."
(Matthew 2:15, MKJV)

Triumphal entry riding on a colt

When Jesus finally came into Jerusalem to suffer at the hands of mankind, it was prophesied that He would ride on a donkey, a colt.

"Rejoice greatly, O daughter of Zion; shout, O daughter of Jerusalem; behold, your King comes to you. He is righteous and victorious, meek and riding on an ass, even on a colt, the son of an ass."
(Zechariah 9:9, MKJV)

This happened as foretold:

"And they brought the colt to Jesus, and they threw their garments on it. And He sat on it.
And many spread their garments in the way, and others cut down branches off the trees and scattered them in the way.
And those going before, and those following, cried out, saying, Hosanna! Blessed is He who comes in the name of the Lord!
Blessed is the kingdom of our father David, who comes in the name of the Lord! Hosanna in the highest!"
(Mark 11:7-10, MKJV)

Betrayed for thirty pieces of silver

It was foretold that a close friend would betray Jesus for exactly thirty pieces of silver.

Zechariah was playing out the betrayal of Jesus, in which similar events happened:

"And it was broken in that day; and so the poor of the flock who were watching Me knew that it was the Word of Jehovah.
And I said to them, If it is good, give My price; and if not, let it go. So they weighed My price thirty pieces of silver.
And Jehovah said to me, Throw it to the potter, the magnificent price at which I was valued by them. And I took the thirty pieces of silver and threw them to the potter in the house of Jehovah."
(Zechariah 11:11-13, MKJV)

And this was also the price for Jesus:

"Then one of the twelve, called Judas Iscariot, went to the chief priests.
And he said to them, What will you give me, and I will betray Him to you? And they appointed to him thirty pieces of silver.
And from that time he sought opportunity to betray Him."
(Matthew 26:14-16, MKJV)

Soldiers gambling for His garments

King David was granted insights into the way mankind would treat the Son of God. He wrote a psalm that indicates the horrible way people can be. One behavior trait was that soldiers would gamble for His garments after His death:

"They divide My garments among them and cast lots for My clothing."
(Psalms 22:18, MKJV)

This also actually happened:

"And coming to a place called Golgotha, which is called, Place of a Skull,
they gave Him vinegar mixed with gall to drink. And when He had tasted, He would not drink.
And they crucified Him, dividing His garments, casting a lot; so that it might be fulfilled which was spoken by the prophet, "They parted My garments among them, and they cast a lot for My clothing."
(Matthew 27:33-35, MKJV)

Heir to the throne of David

Jesus obeyed and achieved the ascendance to the throne granted by God to His earthly leader.

"For to us a Child is born, to us a Son is given; and the government shall be on His shoulder; and His name shall be called Wonderful, Counselor, The mighty God, The everlasting Father, The Prince of Peace.
There is no end of the increase of His government and peace on the throne of David, and on His kingdom, to order it and to establish it with judgment and with justice from now on, even forever. The zeal of Jehovah of Hosts will do this.
(Isaiah 9:6-7, MKJV)

The events were set in motion at Christ's first advent, as was explained to Mary by the angel of God.

"And behold! You shall conceive in your womb and bear a son, and you shall call His name JESUS.
He shall be great and shall be called the Son of the Highest. And the Lord God shall give Him the throne of His father David.
And He shall reign over the house of Jacob forever, and of His kingdom there shall be no end.
(Luke 1:30-33, MKJV)

This was fulfilled in Jesus, by supernatural power!

Galilean ministry

Isaiah, the prophet, indicated that Christ would begin His ministry from the area of Galilee.

"Yet there will be no gloom for her who was in anguish, as in the former time. He degraded the land of Zebulun, and the land of Naphtali, so afterwards He will glorify the way of the sea, beyond Jordan, Galilee of the nations. The people who walked in darkness have seen a great light; they who dwell in the land of the shadow of death, on them the light has shined."
(Isaiah 9:1-2, MKJV)

This is what Jesus did. He started His ministry from the very towns mentioned, exactly as prophesied!

"But when Jesus heard that John was thrown into prison, He went back into Galilee.
And leaving Nazareth, He came and lived in Capernaum, which is on the seacoast, in the borders of Zebulun and Naphtali,
so that it might be fulfilled which was spoken by Isaiah the prophet, saying,
"The land of Zebulun and the land of Naphtali, by way of the sea, beyond Jordan, Galilee of the nations!
The people who sat in darkness saw a great Light; and Light has sprung up to those who sat in the region and shadow of death."
From that time Jesus began to preach and to say, Repent! For the kingdom of Heaven is at hand."
(Matthew 4:12-17, MKJV)

From Galilee, Jesus received supporters and disciples, as God's Holy Spirit led Him, and motivated the future apostles. It was here where most of His miracles happened, as prophesied!

"And walking by the Sea of Galilee, Jesus saw two brothers, Simon called Peter, and Andrew his brother, casting a net into the sea. For they were fishermen.
And He said to them, Follow Me, and I will make you fishers of men.
And they immediately left their nets and followed him.
And going on from there, he saw another two brothers, James the son of Zebedee, and John his brother, in a boat with Zebedee their father, mending their nets. And He called them;
and they immediately left the boat and their father and followed Him.
And Jesus went about all Galilee, teaching in their synagogues and preaching the gospel of the kingdom, and healing all kinds of sickness and all kinds of disease among the people."
(Matthew 4:18-23, MKJV)

Speaks in parables

A surprising aspect of Jesus' ministry was that he often spoke in parables.

"I will open my mouth in a parable; I will speak dark sayings of old,"
(Psalm 78:2, MKJV)

This is what Jesus did, as foretold. He employed the technique often to bring the message home to the minds of people. It is a fascinating technique. Those that have enough knowledge will understand. It will make sense to those that are interested in the Kingdom of God, and which have studied and learned before. The message will stick in their minds, as it takes some thinking to resolve the otherwise mysterious message.

For those who have no background knowledge and could possibly be antagonistic to the message, it would not make sense. They would either have to seek insights from the true followers honestly or else leave without gaining new knowledge.

"Jesus spoke all these things to the crowds in parables, and He did not speak to them without a parable,"
(Matthew 13:34)

This technique is protective of the message and those that gladly understand and accept it with joy.

Bind up the broken hearted

Sin leads to misery. Their sin captures them. People are hurt. It breeds further hurt, even crime. Somehow the cycle needs to be broken. This is one of the goals for the Messiah.

"The Spirit of the Lord Jehovah is on Me; because Jehovah has anointed Me to preach the Gospel to the poor; He has sent Me to bind up the broken-hearted, to proclaim liberty to the captives, and the opening of the prison to those who are bound;
to preach the acceptable year of Jehovah and the day of vengeance of our God; to comfort all who mourn;
(Isaiah 61:102, MKJV)

Jesus knew this was one of His goals. He achieved this when He came. He read this scripture to the people to explain one of His missions:

"The Spirit of the Lord is on Me; because of this He has anointed Me to proclaim the Gospel to the poor. He has sent me to heal the brokenhearted, to proclaim deliverance to the captives, and new sight to the blind, to set at liberty those having been crushed,
to proclaim the acceptable year of the Lord."
(Luke 4:16-19, MKJV)

The exact way is explained in another book called "Fulfillment of the Sin sacrifice"

Adored by infants

Preconceived ideas do not burden children. They don't care about the status quo. They will declare something the way they see it. However, the strength of the faith and conviction is often prevented by old and sometimes misplaced concepts.

"Out of the mouths of babes and sucklings You have ordained strength, because of ones vexing You, to cause the enemy and the avenger to cease."
(Psalm 8:2, MKJV)

While the Pharisees and Sadducees worked to prevent Jesus, children saw things as they are, and were not hindered in their praise.

"And when the chief priests and scribes saw the wonderful things which He did, and the children crying in the temple, and saying, Hosanna to the Son of David, they were angry.
And they said to Him, Do you hear what these say? And Jesus said to them, Yes, have you never read, "Out of the mouth of babes and sucklings You have perfected praise?"
(Matthew 21:15-16, MKJV)

Crucified with criminals

Christ had to be our High Priest, as well as our Sin Offering. He fulfilled both roles for our salvation.

Firstly He suffered at our hands, dying the death that we deserved. We should understand from this how bad we really are. The reasons are explained in another eBook: "Fulfillment of the Sin Sacrifice.

Secondly, He had to suffer our sin with patience and love, proving to be the perfect go-between. He loved us while dying on the crucifix. He also loved His heavenly Father, even though this was required of Him by His Father. It did not upset Him. He achieved perfect love both ways.

"Therefore I will divide to Him with the great, and He shall divide the spoil with the strong; because He has poured out His soul to death; and He was counted among the transgressors; and He bore the sin of many, and made intercession for transgressors."
(Isaiah 53:12, MKJV)

Jesus Christ performed this out of love for His Father as well as humankind.

"And with Him they crucified two thieves, the one off the right, and one off the left.
And the Scripture was fulfilled which said, "And he was numbered with the lawless."
(Mark 15:27-28, MKJV)

Prayed for His enemies

Jesus love for people extended to His enemies. He would even pray for them! His loving ways were foretold:

"For my love they are my foes; but I am in prayer."
(Psalms 109:4, MKJV)

And that is what He did:

"And Jesus said, Father, forgive them, for they do not know what they do. And parting His clothing, they cast lots."
(Luke 23:34, MKJV)

Even in His darkest hour He still prayed for His enemies!

Pierced to die

Jesus Christ died a horrible denigrating death!

"And I will pour on the house of David, and on the people of Jerusalem, the spirit of grace and of prayers. And they shall look on Me whom they have pierced, and they shall mourn for Him, as one mourns for his only son, and shall be bitter over Him, as the bitterness over the first-born."
(Zechariah 12:10, MKJV)

The people will understand how terrible Jesus, the Son of God, was treated. This will lead to heart-rendering repentance.

"But one of the soldiers pierced His side with a lance, and instantly there came out blood and water."
(john 19:34, MKJV)

There are many more prophecies about Him that Jesus Christ fulfilled. Some scholars list over 300 prophecies. Most of these cannot be planned and arranged by a single earthy individual. Many were out of His control, and some happened when He was an infant. It could not have been arranged by men. It can only be a miracle. Only with God's continuous intervention could this have happened on such a large scale.

Indeed, Jesus Christ was the Greatest Prophet of God!

Chapter 5

Did Christ change everything?

We have seen in the scriptures that no prophet can come and drastically change the worship, and do away with the established Godly order. No prophet can disregard the Law outright and expect to be followed, except by people who have not had the fortune of being properly trained.

"And many false prophets will rise and deceive many." (Matthew 24:11, MKJV)

So Jesus warned that many false prophets would come after Him. They would go against the law and the writings of the old prophets.

Some may view some groups in Christianity that appears to have has drifted away from the original Faith. Then it seems as though Jesus did just that!

Is it true? If so, does it not disqualify Jesus as a prophet of God?

This is a serious accusation and often brought up by adherents of other faiths. We need to deal with this in some depth.

What has changed? How has it changed? When did it change? Was the change correct? Was the change foretold in the old prophecies? Is it acceptable before God?

To answer these questions, we will do a quick tour of the history of Christianity, and ask some serious questions.

We will see that popular Christianity may have drifted too far. Popular and charismatic Christianity may have made a mistake of putting forth an incorrect image or concept of Jesus. This may be just as problematic as other faiths that follow other prophets that claim to be real but fails the test of the old scriptures.

Quick overview of Christian history

We will give a quick overview for reference. The reader can do research in any library and will find this to be factual. An Internet search for names will also prove this.

In the first century after the Crucifixion, Christianity spread across Asia and into the Roman Empire. Pagan religious groups were obviously quite upset, and would have brought accusations against Christians. Remember also that there was a Jewish revolt against Roman occupation in Jerusalem that resulted in the destruction of the Temple. The Roman Emperor Nero afterwards rather hated the Jews and by extension the Christians. There are reports that he caused Christians to be burned! However Christianity could not be stopped, as it was from God.

In the fourth century another Roman Emperor Constantine decided to make peace between the Christians and other pagan religions. He did what a typical politician would do. He brokered a compromise. He formed councils in which bishops from Rome and other areas could bring submissions to debate Christian doctrine. The first was the Council of Nicaea. What has happened over the centuries was that false preachers that were former pagan preachers had entered the Christian fold and had begun mixing true doctrine with pagan concepts.

Saturday Sabbath to Sunday

For instance, the Saturday Sabbath was changed to worship on Sundays. Also Saturnalia on 25 December was converted to Xmas. The belief in pagan triune belief systems merged with the belief in the Father and the Son, and combined with making the Spirit of God into a third person, and changed to the belief of the Triune God. Ancestor worship was combined with the belief in the resurrection, and what emerged was the idea that when we die, we immediately go to heaven, apparently satisfying both apostate Christians and pagans. Many books were written on these processes. Apparently,

Constantine became a "Christian" himself shortly before his death. However he accepted the modified Christianity that he brokered between different religions.

Christian apostasy

These facts may be a shock to the average reader, but the purpose here is to show that the Christianity that eventually emerged after the third council was quite different from first-century Christianity. A lot was changed by apostate leaders. It was quite a departure from what Jesus intended. Notice what the apostle said towards the end of the first century:

"Having made all haste to write to you about the common salvation, beloved, I had need to write to you to exhort you to contend earnestly for the faith once delivered to the saints.
For certain men crept in secretly, those having been of old previously written into this condemnation, ungodly ones perverting the grace of our God for unbridled lust, and denying the only Master, God, even our Lord Jesus Christ."
(Jude 1:3-4, MKJV)

The apostasy had already started in the first century. By the fourth century, it was complete. What we had in the fourth century and beyond were a modified Christianity that even Emperor Constantine could accept.

However, it was an apostate Christianity that had changed things. The bishops from Rome then used the power of the Roman state to enforce the modified Christianity.

From the sixth century, Europe entered the period known in history as the Dark Middle Ages. This lasted for about 1260 years until the Reformation came as per the prophecy. The reformation mainly started when Martin Luther King nailed a list of errors on the door of a Roman church.

New technology brought the printed press, and the Bible was now accessible to ordinary citizens and scholars. Thanks to Wycliffe and others, the Bible was available in English, and ordinary citizens could read for themselves, and discover just how far Christianity had drifted away.

These Dark Middle Ages were actually prophesied by Daniel the prophet. In a general overview of the past two thousand years, Daniel wrote the following:

"And he shall speak words against the Most High, and shall wear out the saints of the Most High, and plot to change times and laws. And they shall be given into his hand until a time and times and one-half time." (Daniel 7:25, MKJV)

The description of "time, times and one half time" can prophetically be calculated as follows: A time is a prophetic year of 360 days. This is accepted by scholars but is also explained in the eBook "The Flood – can we believe it?"

Every day then forms a year in history. By adding it all up, we arrive at 1260 years, the length of the Dark Middle Ages. The main aspect of this period was that a certain ruler changed times and laws of the worship of God through Christ, and the saints would have great difficulty continuing the true worship in the face of a civil ruler that would try and enforce his alterations onto the true worshippers. We know that this was the Roman Emperor Constantine in the fourth century.

Through Jesus, the Prophet, the same was repeated in the book of Revelation. See Revelation 1:1-2. The prophecy was shown again in Revelation 12, where the true worshippers were granted a way of escape from persecution.

We must understand that rule of the Roman Empire at that time was oppressive, leading to the crucifixion of the Son of God. In the Dark Middle Ages the small flock of true believers was eventually given a way of escape to their free worlds:

"And two wings of a great eagle were given to the woman, so that she might fly into the wilderness, into her place, where she is nourished for a time and times and half a time, from the serpent's face."
(Revelation 12:14, MKJV)

This shows how the true worshippers could flee from persecution to the "free worlds" to form governments where Christian religious freedom was established and enshrined in their constitutions.

From the 16th century, the Reformation blazed forth mainly from the British Isles, and England mainly became Protestant Christian. However, there was strife over just how far the purification should go. King James then brought out the famous King James Version of the Bible, which still contained debatable translation of some verses.

The Sabbatarian Christians who followed a more pure form of Christianity fled Rome and persecution in Europe by going to countries like South Africa, Australia, New Zeeland, and North America. Once they made these areas more livable and had established the rule of law, and freedom of religion for various Christian beliefs, others followed from Europe, and Protestant Christianity became the dominant Faith in these areas.

Changes not made by Jesus

Why are we mentioning these things? The purpose is simply to demonstrate that Christianity in various areas of the world differ depending on historical events and influences.

One cannot say that Jesus made these changes. Men made these changes. Emperor Constantine enforced these changes. In places like Ireland wars were fought over these changes. This is the error of men, not Jesus Christ. Jesus, the Greatest Prophet, did not make all these changes! We cannot say Jesus changed from the Sabbath to Sunday. Jesus did not change the Law and moved away from the Prophets of old!

However, some things did change with the spread of Christianity beyond the promised land of Israel. First century Christianity was different outside Judea. How was it different? What changed to the New Testament era? And was the change sanctioned by the Law and the Prophets? We will investigate in the next chapter.

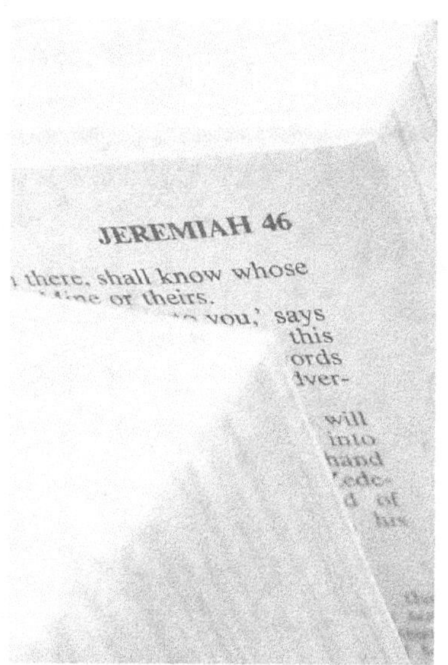
JEREMIAH 46
there, shall know whose
or theirs.
you,' says
this
ords
ver-
will
into
hand
ede-
of
his

Chapter 6

What change was prophesied?

From the Law and the Prophets of old, the coming of the Greatest Prophet was not only prophesied but also that He would change certain aspects of worship. Jesus did not function outside His mandate from God. We will see this as we continue to discover the actual flow of events, and the covenants with God's people through the ages.

Some of the original disciples of Jesus that became apostles may have been poor fishermen, but they were educated in the scriptures. They attended worship services in the synagogues every Sabbath, Holy Days, and New Moons. They were further educated by John the Baptist, and hence they did recognize the Messiah when He came.

"Now Philip was of Bethsaida, the city of Andrew and Peter.
Philip found Nathanael and said to him, We have found Him of whom Moses wrote in the Law and the Prophets, Jesus of Nazareth, the son of Joseph."
(John 1:44-45, MKJV)

There were hundreds of indications all over the Law and Prophets that pointed to Jesus. Those that knew the scriptures were expecting Him and recognized that He was the Messiah. There was no doubt.

So did Jesus come to do a complete break with the scriptures and start a new religion?

"Do not think that I have come to destroy the Law or the Prophets. I have not come to destroy but to fulfill.
For truly I say to you, Till the heaven and the earth pass away, not one jot or one tittle shall in any way pass from the Law until all is fulfilled.
Therefore whoever shall relax one of these commandments, the least, and shall teach men so, he shall be called the least in the kingdom of Heaven. But whoever shall do and teach them, the same shall be called great in the kingdom of Heaven."
(Matthew 5:17-19, MKJV)

Jesus did not come to make a clean break with the Law and the Prophets. He could not change things that were not promised or prophesied to change. If He did, He would have been a false prophet. Israel would have had to reject Him. But Jesus did not do that. He continued in the Law, and He fulfilled prophecies.

Jesus even told the Israelites that they should continue in the Law of Moses:

"And behold, a leper came and worshiped him, saying, Lord, if You will, You can make me clean.
And Jesus put out His hand and touched him, saying, I will; be clean! And immediately his leprosy was cleansed.

And Jesus said to him, See that you tell no one; but go, show yourself to the priest. And offer the gift that Moses commanded, for a testimony to them."
(Matthew 8:2-4, MKJV)

So Jesus did not come to make a clean break and begin a totally new religion. He became the supreme Sacrifice. Even aspects of the Law of Moses continued in this regard.

However, He came to fulfill some Law and prophecies. When they were fulfilled, they were no longer required.

Sacrificial system fulfilled

One particular aspect that was fulfilled was the sacrificial system. Jesus became the ultimate and supreme sacrifice for all people and for all time. No longer would the Passover lamb be sacrificed, nor any other physical sacrifices.

"Your boasting is not good. Do you not know that a little leaven leavens the whole lump?
Therefore purge out the old leaven so that you may be a new lump, as you are unleavened. For also Christ our Passover is sacrificed for us.
Therefore let us keep the feast; not with old leaven, nor with the leaven of malice and wickedness, but with the unleavened bread of sincerity and truth."
(1 Corinthians 5:6-8, MKJV)

Jesus Christ became the final and perfect sacrifice and fulfilled that law, but keeping the Holy Days continued. Hence no longer will animal sacrifices be done. To do so would be an affront to Almighty God. To sacrifice any animal is to say to God that the crucifixion of His Son was not good enough!

Sacrificing animals stopped with the Sacrifice of Jesus Christ.

Sacrificing was brought into worship during the Exodus as a temporary measure to keep the covenant intact. But it was not the best measure.

"For the Law which has a shadow of good things to come, not the very image of the things, appearing year by year with the same sacrifices, which they offer continually, they are never able to perfect those drawing near.
For then would they not have ceased to be offered? Because the worshipers, when they had been once for all purged, would have had no more conscience of sin.
But in those sacrifices there is a remembrance again of sins every year.
For it is not possible that the blood of bulls and of goats should take away sins.
Therefore when He comes into the world, He says,
"Sacrifice and offering You did not desire, but You have prepared a body for Me.
In burnt offerings and sacrifices for sin You have had no pleasure.

Then I said, Lo, I come (in the volume of the Book it is written of Me) to do Your will, O God."
Above, when He said, "Sacrifice and offering, and burnt offerings and offering for sin You did not desire, neither did You have pleasure in them" (which are offered according to the Law),
then He said, "Lo, I come to do Your will, O God." He takes away the first so that He may establish the second."
(Hebrews 10:1-9, MKJV)

The apostle is quoting from the Psalms a piece of prophecy. So this change that Jesus brought was prophesied. It was not something completely new. It was in line with God's Will from the beginning.

Change in priesthood

A further aspect was the priesthood. In the Exodus, the sons of Levi were made priests for the service of the Temple.

"then Moses stood in the gate of the camp and said, Who is on Jehovah's side? Come to me. And all the sons of Levi gathered themselves to him."
(Exodus 32:26, MKJV)

From this time, priests could only come from the Levites:

"And Jehovah spoke to Moses saying,

Bring the tribe of Levi near, and present them before
Aaron the priest, so that they may minister to him.
And they shall keep his charge and the charge of the
whole congregation before the tabernacle of the
congregation, to do the service of the tabernacle."
(Numbers 3:5-7, MKJV)

This was a temporary measure due to the sin in the
desert. However, Jesus came to restore the worship
according to the priesthood of Melchizedek.

"And if I may say so, Levi, also, who receives tithes,
paid tithes in Abraham.
For he was still in the loins of his father when
Melchizedek met him.
Therefore if perfection were by the Levitical priesthood
(for under it the people received the Law), what further
need was there that another priest should rise after the
order of Melchizedek, and not be called after the order of
Aaron?
For the priesthood being changed, there is of necessity a
change made in the law also.
For He of whom these things are spoken belongs to
another tribe, from which no man gave attendance at the
altar.
For it is evident that our Lord sprang out of Judah, of
which tribe Moses spoke nothing concerning priesthood.
And it is still far more evident, since there arises another
priest after the likeness of Melchizedek,
who is made, not according to the law of a fleshly
commandment, but according to the power of an endless
life.

For He testifies, "You are a priest forever after the order
of Melchizedek."
For truly there is a putting away of the commandment
which went before, because of the weakness and
unprofitableness of it.
For the Law made nothing perfect, but the bringing in of
a better hope did, by which we draw near to God.
And inasmuch as He was not made priest without an
oath
(for those priests were made without an oath, but this
one was made with an oath by Him who said to Him,
"The Lord swore and will not repent, You are a priest
forever after the order of Melchizedek,")"
(Hebrew 7:9-21

Hence Jesus actually did not do something new. He was
simply restoring what existed before Moses and what
was implemented during the Exodus.

"And Melchizedek the king of Salem brought forth bread
and wine. And he was the priest of the most high God.
And he blessed him, and said, Blessed be Abram of the
most high God, possessor of Heaven and earth.
And blessed be the most high God, who has delivered
your enemies into your hand. And he gave him tithes of
all."
(Genesis 14:18-20, MKJV)

Easy divorce

We can also see other aspects of how Jesus did not change things but restored things to the way it was before, the way God wanted it initially.

"And tempting Him, the Pharisees came to Him and asked Him, Is it lawful for a man to put away his wife?
And He answered and said to them, What did Moses command you?
And they said, Moses allowed a bill of divorce to be written, and to put her away.
And Jesus answered and said to them, He wrote you this precept because of the hardness of your hearts.
But from the beginning of the creation God made them male and female.
For this cause a man shall leave his father and mother and shall cleave to his wife.
And the two of them shall be one flesh. So then they are no longer two, but one flesh."
(Mark 10:2-8, MKJV)

Moses allowed easy divorce, for the men were hard in their ways, thereby reducing women to poverty. But God did not want it that way, and Jesus restored the man's responsibility.

Ten Commandments still in force

The Ten Commandments are still in force. The reason is elevated. The motivation has changed. The ability is now spiritual.

"not according to the covenant that I made with their fathers in the day I took hold of their hand to lead them out of the land of Egypt," because they did not continue in My covenant, and I did not regard them, says the Lord.
 "For this is the covenant that I will make with the house of Israel after those days, says the Lord: I will put My Laws into their mind and write them in their hearts, and I will be their God, and they shall be My people."
(Hebrews 8:9-10, MKJV)

Some Law continues. Jesus did not start something completely new. Notice how He explained to the Jews how the Commandments continue:

"You have heard that it was said to the ancients, "You shall not kill" --and, "Whoever shall kill shall be liable to the judgment."
But I say to you that whoever is angry with his brother without a cause shall be liable to the judgment. And whoever shall say to his brother, Raca, shall be liable to the sanhedrin; but whoever shall say, Fool! shall be liable to be thrown into the fire of hell."
(Matthew 5:21-22, MKJV)

Jesus made the Commandments more binding by raising obedience to the spiritual level.

Restoring original worship

We can see in several ways how Jesus restored the original worship. When He came, it was time to renew the original worship. Some aspects of the Law of Moses came because former slave people coming out of Egypt had to be controlled. It was a tall order for them to come out of paganism and reach out to full spiritual worship. Hence God allowed more ritualistic worship to keep the nation together. However, the physical ritual was always designed to point to a spiritual reality. It pictured the workings of a true relationship between humanity and the God of heaven, through a high priest.

Space prohibits a comprehensive study in what changed during Christ's ministry, and why it changed. In many ways, some things were restored to the way it was with Abraham, Isaac, and Jacob. The book of Hebrews is actually a treaty to the Hebrew people to explain the changes.

The point of this chapter is to argue the point that Jesus did not come to make a new religion. It was a continuation of what was promised from the beginning.

The Ten Commandments were evident before the Exodus of Israel and incorporated. Jesus did not do away with them. Jesus did away with animal sacrifices, and other aspects were restored to how it was before Moses.

Today in the free world, Christian churches may differ in the exact level of reformation and restoration. But Christians must understand that Jesus Christ did not bring a new religion. Some apostasy has taken many away from true worship. That has led many to assume Jesus made a total break and started a totally new religion. In reality, that is not the case.

Circumcision to be an Israelite

One further aspect is that Circumcision and its related laws are not required. The worship at the Physical Temple in Jerusalem would not be possible for worshippers far away on the other side of the world. The apostles discussed this issue:

"And certain ones who came down from Judea taught
the brothers, saying, Unless you are circumcised
according to the custom of Moses, you cannot be saved."
(Acts 15:1, MKJV)

This was an issue that had to be addressed! Was it a requirement for Christians in the whole world to become Israelites through circumcision? Notice the discussion, and how scriptures were quoted to back the decision. It was not something new. It was already decided long ago:

"Even as Simon has declared how God at the first visited the nations to take out of them a people for His name.
And the words of the Prophets agree to this; as it is written,
"After this I will return and will build again the tabernacle of David which has fallen down; and I will build again its ruins, and I will set it up,
so those men who are left might seek after the Lord, and all the nations on whom My name has been called, says the Lord, who does all these things."
(Acts 15:14-17, MKJV)

Christians do not have to be circumcised to become Israelites in order to receive salvation. This was not something new. It was decided long ago.

Jesus fulfilled what was defined for Him long before. His apostles also followed the scriptures. It cannot be said that He changed everything and made a new religion. The few changes were prophesied before. Hence Jesus fulfilled the criteria to be a true Prophet. He was the Greatest Prophet.

Chapter 7

Denying Christ's superiority

Some people may deny that Jesus Christ is the only begotten Son of God. Many deny that He is alive and is currently at the right hand of God. Some may deny that He is our High Priest with God, interceding on our behalf, by proposing the Trinity Doctrine. Some may even deny the need for such a Supreme Being to be our savior.

Is our heavenly Father happy with this?

During the transfiguration on the mount, Jesus was allowing Peter to experience a vision of the future Kingdom of God. In the Kingdom, Moses and Elijah would be resurrected and will be with Jesus, assisting in the affairs of the Kingdom. During that event, almighty God gave us a very clear indication of who He favored, and who we must follow and obey.

"But I tell you truly, there are some standing here who shall not taste of death until they see the kingdom of God.
And about eight days after these sayings, He took Peter and John and James and went up into a mountain to pray. And as He prayed, the appearance of His countenance was altered, and His clothing was dazzling white.

And behold, two men talked with Him, who were Moses
and Elijah,
who appeared in glory and spoke of His exodus, which
He was about to accomplish at Jerusalem.
But Peter and those with him were heavy with sleep. But
fully awakening, they saw His glory, and the two men
who stood with Him.
And in their parting from Him, it happened that Peter
said to Jesus, Master, it is good for us to be here. And let
us make three tabernacles, one for You and one for
Moses and one for Elijah; not knowing what he said.
And as he was saying these things, a cloud came and
overshadowed them. And they feared as they entered
into the cloud.
And a voice came out of the cloud, saying, This is My
Son, the Beloved, hear Him."
(Luke 9:27-35, MKJV)

Jesus is the beloved Son of God. We must hear Him.
God will allow salvation and blessings through His Son.

This was promised to Abraham long ago:

"And the Angel of Jehovah called to Abraham out of the
heavens the second time,
and said, I have sworn by Myself, says Jehovah; because
you have done this thing, and have not withheld your
son, your only one;
that in blessing I will bless you, and in multiplying I will
multiply your seed like the stars of the heavens, and as
the sand which is upon the seashore. And your Seed
shall possess the gate of His enemies.

And in your Seed shall all the nations of the earth be blessed, because you have obeyed My voice."
(Genesis 22:15-18, MKJV)

The Seed of Abraham through which the nations would be blessed was Jesus Christ:

"so that the blessing of Abraham might be to the nations in Jesus Christ, and that we might receive the promise of the Spirit through faith.
Brothers, I speak according to man, a covenant having been ratified, even among mankind, no one sets aside or adds to it.
And to Abraham and to his Seed the promises were spoken. It does not say, And to seeds, as of many; but as of one, "And to your Seed," which is Christ."
(Galatians 3:14-16, MKJV)

Peace and prosperity, and knowledge and understanding of the Kingdom of God come through Jesus Christ. Those that reject Jesus as the only begotten Son of God may lose out on peace and prosperity but, in particular, salvation. This is the way it is. Almighty God has decided this. Who are we to argue?

When paganism entered the Christian churches in the first century, the apostles were horrified to understand that some would formulate an apostate religion that would deny the relationship between the Most High God and His Son. They would deny the loving relationship, and the favor Jesus carries with God the Father. They would deny Jesus' preexistence. They would deny His power and right to forgive sins, a power granted by God if we repent.

Such people have a big problem. They must then obey every aspect of Law of Moses perfectly or be condemned. Forgiveness is not in them. They will also not forgive others on true repentance and restoration, but expect harsh punishment, because they have not been forgiven, and cannot make a new start. They are in a difficult and pitiful situation.

"For God so loved the world that He gave His only-begotten Son, that whoever believes in Him should not perish but have everlasting life.
For God did not send His Son into the world to condemn the world, but so that the world might be saved through Him.
He who believes on Him is not condemned, but he who does not believe is condemned already, because he has not believed in the name of the only-begotten Son of God."
(John 3:16, MKJV)

Those that will not receive the preexistent and only begotten Son of God do not expect forgiveness when repentant and stays under condemnation. It is a terrible way to be. It brings strife and war, for they will not forgive when there is repentance, and demand harsh punishment even when the offenders are repentant, and yet they feel and know that they are not forgiven. It is impossible to live and learn and build under such a heavy yoke. They don't have a clear way to make things right with God.

The only way to make things right with God is through our Lord and Savior Jesus the Christ, our compassionate High Priest in Heaven, the Greatest Prophet of all time!

Chapter 8

The next prophet

After the time of Jesus Christ's first advent - and His guidance, commandments, wisdom, and prophecies He gave through His apostles - no further major prophet is expected, till shortly before His second advent. Nobody can come and make major changes. The changes foretold in the Old Testament scriptures were done by Jesus Christ at during his Ministry of his First Advent.

Nobody can go and add a big volume of revised instructions on top of the book of Revelation. The body of knowledge required for life and salvation is complete. Any person that does so can be in trouble with God.

Notice His instructions given at the end of Revelation:

"For I testify together to everyone who hears the Words of the prophecy of this Book: If anyone adds to these things, God will add on him the plagues that have been written in this Book.
And if anyone takes away from the Words of the Book of this prophecy, God will take away his part out of the Book of Life, and out of the holy city, and from the things which have been written in this Book."
(Revelation 22:18-19, MKJV)

Does this warning only apply to the book of Revelation, or the Bible?

If it only applies to the book of Revelation, it does not make sense. Any new person claiming to be a new prophet will add a new book. This then renders the warning obsolete. Then it has little or no effect. The book of Revelation was set about two thousand years ago, and billions of copies have spread across the world. It was not physically possible to add to the book of Revelation even a short hundred years after it was written.

So it must apply to the whole message of the Bible. Only then it has an effect for hundreds to thousands of years till Christ's Second Advent.

This means that nobody can add another book that is different, claiming to depart new knowledge and be considered a great prophet of God. Such a person and followers are in danger of suffering the bad things written in Revelation. It includes drought, wars, destruction of communities, and various calamities.

We are advised that the sum total of words is sealed up. Jesus was the final Great Prophet that was promised. Nobody else is required for salvation.

"Do not labor for the food that perishes, but for that food which endures to everlasting life, which the Son of Man will give you. For God, the Father sealed Him.

Then they said to Him, What shall we do that we might work the works of God?
Jesus answered and said to them, This is the work of God, that you believe on Him whom He has sent.
(John 6:27-29, MKJV)

Salvation and eternal life are sealed in Jesus Christ and His ministry. No further great prophet will come, except in the End Time, in the Last Days.

Expecting "Elijah"

What we are expecting is a prophet that will come at the end time, in the Last Days. This was prophesied in the Old Testament:

"Behold, I am sending you Elijah the prophet before the coming of the great and dreadful day of Jehovah.
And he shall turn the heart of the fathers to the sons, and the heart of the sons to their fathers, that I not come and strike the earth with utter destruction."
(Malachi 4:5-6, MKJV)

When Jesus came the first time, He could have been the leader that freed Israel. It could have been a salvation for all. But God knew that humanity and even the Jews were sinners, and the Sanhedrin under the Pharisees had hidden agendas and would not follow Christ. So Christ had to deal with the sinfulness of humankind and allow people to kill Him. This led to the greatest public repentance, where thousands of people repented after

Peter's sermon. Enough people had to be converted and needed to be trained and had to be repentant for the Kingdom to be established. This was not the case at the first Advent.

Hence another prophet needs to come in the mold and spirit of Elijah just before Christ's Second Advent to prepare the way again as John the Baptist did. This leads to what is seen in the scriptures as dual prophecy, where prior events will happen again. The foolishness of humanity needs to be judged in wars before humanity will yearn for Messiah to return to clean up the mess and prevent the annihilation of humanity.

Speaking of the future, Jesus said the following:

"And His disciples asked Him, saying, Why then do the
scribes say that Elijah must come first?
And answering Jesus said to them, Elijah truly shall
come first and restore all things.
But I say to you that Elijah has come already, and they
did not know him, but have done to him whatever they
desired. Likewise also the Son of Man shall suffer from
them."
(Matthew 17:10-12, MKJV)

So the expectation is for another prophet to come in the spirit of Elijah, just like John the Baptist.

How would we know that this final prophet came? How will we identify him?

For one thing, we know that he will still be alive when Christ's Second Advent occurs. All people that claimed to be that prophet but have died are obviously not that prophet.

What are the indications of that final prophet? We can look back at John the Baptist and find some indications.

We know that religious leaders sometimes drift off the mark. We have seen that even in the days of the original apostles, the apostasy already began. From history books we can see how the Roman Emperor Constantine worked a diplomatic truce between Christianity and pagan religions in his empire and so corrupted Christianity. What we see that general popular Christianity today is sometimes removed from the original faith.

The general public of today may not even recognize Jesus if He returns right now. If He returns, the armies of the world will think it is an alien invasion, and they will fight Him! He will not be what they expect. He may be different than what they were led to believe. He will not be a weak long haired soft person with soft words. He will be a strong uncompromising leader, who comes in power and authority.

"And I saw the beast, and the kings of the earth and their armies, being gathered to make war against Him who sat on the horse, and against His army."
(Revelation 19:19, MKJV)

Hence the prophet that comes in the spirit of Elijah will restore the true worship and gain enough followers to fill up the sum of true believers that are required for Christ to provide leadership at His Second Advent.

From several scriptures, we can see that this final prophet will do his ministry right at the end before Christ returns. This prophet will restore things that were lost through the past two millennia of Christianity. World leaders and even some churches will not sway him. And he will not make big claims to be that prophet. He will be humble before God. Only the returned Christ will acknowledge him as before, and then he will admit that he was indeed that final prophet that came in the spirit of Elijah because Christ said so.

To enable people to identify this prophet, they will have to do an in-depth study of their Bibles. They will have to research the original Faith, and purify their lives. The rest of the people will be unaware or unsure of his existence until shortly before the end.

He may have the power to prevent rain, as Elijah did. He may challenge religious leaders directly, as Elijah did. But the world, in general, will not be able to identify him, nor be willing to follow him.

Chapter 9

The Two Witnesses

Our study will not be complete without a discussion of the final Two Witnesses.

In the book of Revelation mention is made of the final Two Witnesses. Who are they? What will they do? Let's look at the scriptures:

"And a reed like a rod was given to me. And the angel stood, saying, Rise up and measure the temple of God, and the altar, and those who worship in it.
But leave out the court which is outside the temple, and do not measure it, for it was given to the nations. And they will trample the holy city forty-two months.
And I will give power to My two witnesses, and they will prophesy a thousand, two hundred and sixty days, clothed in sackcloth."
(Revelation 11:1-3, MKJV)

At this stage, we must understand that the temple refers to the Church of God, as the apostle Paul shows us:

"Do you not know that you are a temple of God, and that the Spirit of God dwells in you?"
(1 Corinthians 3:16, MKJV)

This change from the physical temple was one of the legitimate changes brought on by Jesus Christ. His sacrifice was in accordance with the Law and superseded the Old Covenant, and its animal sacrifices:

"and said, This one said, I am able to destroy the temple of God and to build it in three days."
(Matthew 26:61, MKJV)

So we understand that the angel is not talking of the physical temple but the Church of God. Hence we need to understand the scriptures in relation to the Church and its effect, and what will happen in the last days before Christ's return.

Two witnesses will arise and challenge the status quo. Nations have drifted. Leaders of countries have disregarded the Scriptures. Even churches have drifted away from the original Faith. Two witnesses will come and set the record straight. They will even be given supernatural power to show that they are true, and the messages are from God. They need to be heard and taken seriously!

But why two witnesses? Let's go back to learn some history, and then consider a vision from God.

When Israel lived in the Promised Land, they drifted and preferred to have a king like other nations around. They rejected the prophet as the only ruler. They wanted to become more secular. They could not reach up to a purely spiritual way of being. They asked for a king.

"And they said to him, Behold, you are old, and your sons do not walk in your ways. Now make us a king to judge us like all the nations.
But the thing was evil in the eyes of Samuel, when they said, Give us a king to judge us. And Samuel prayed to Jehovah.
And Jehovah said to Samuel, Listen to the voice of the people in all that they say to you. For they have not rejected you, but they have rejected Me, that I should not reign over them.
According to all the works which they have done since the day that I brought them up out of Egypt even until this day, works with which they have forsaken Me and served other gods, so they do also to you.
And now listen to their voice. Only, you shall surely protest solemnly to them, and show them the kind of king who shall reign over them."
(1 Samuel 8:5-9, MKJV)

So a new relationship between God and the nation began. There will be two authorities over the nation. One will provide spiritual leadership and the other civil leadership. We see a separation between church and state. These are supposed to work together to lead the nation. This became the norm for many nations for thousands of years. God expects both church and state to give serious consideration to His guidance, but in different spheres of influence and authority. God holds both accountable. The king and the prophet may drift and even disregard God to the demise of the nation, but in the resurrection, they will learn that God still holds them accountable. Hence God will send two witnesses that will speak out against the nations and churches to repent before the coming of Christ the King to which all authority will be given in the end. When Christ returns, church, and state will be united again under Him and not before. So God will arrange for two witnesses to deal with churches and states.

We see this in a vision about the future that Jesus arranged for the apostles during Christ's first advent:

"And after six days Jesus took Peter, James, and John his brother, and brought them up into a high mountain apart. And He was transfigured before them. And His face shone as the sun, and His clothing was white as the light. And behold, there appeared to them Moses and Elijah talking with Him.
And Peter answered and said to Jesus, Lord, it is good for us to be here. If You will, let us make here three tabernacles; one for You, and one for Moses, and one for Elijah.
While he yet spoke, behold, a bright cloud overshadowed them. And behold a voice out of the cloud which said, This is My beloved Son in whom I am well pleased, hear Him.
And when the disciples heard, they fell on their face and were greatly terrified.
And Jesus came and touched them, and said, Arise and do not be terrified.

And lifting up their eyes, they saw no one except Jesus alone."
(Matthew 17:3-8, MKJV)

We see two witnesses here with Jesus, Moses and Elijah. In the previous chapter we looked at someone in the mold of Elijah. But now we also see someone else in the mold of Moses.

Why Moses?

Moses was born when Israel was a slave nation in Egypt. In an oppressed situation, Moses was spared when his mother sent him on the river to protect him from being killed by Faro's soldiers. Moses was seen and collected and was raised in Egypt in the court of Faro. He learned all about government, civil order, and managing a nation. Moses later led Israel out of Egypt to establish the new nation in the Promised Land. Moses received the Commandments and the civil Law from God. With God's blessing, he also added the Law of Moses when Israel sinned greatly in the desert, to reduce sin. Moses knew about nation-building. He was the one who would establish God's nation. He wrote the first five books of the Bible. He was the king of Israel, but initially also the prophet. However, his greatest capability was in the sphere of leading the nation in civil affairs.

Moses represents the civil authority over the nations.

Hence we see the two witnesses in the book of Revelation. They will speak out to the spiritual and civil aspects of nations. Civil and religious leaders and authorities will know they have drifted far from God's guidance, and have caused wars and misery. A warning must go out to both entities to provide an opportunity for repentance before the final holocaust and wars of the end, during which time Christ will return to end the madness.

God will support the two witnesses with supernatural capabilities to make sure the world knows about them and hears their warnings.

"These are the two olive trees and the two lampstands standing before the God of the earth.
And if anyone will hurt them, fire proceeds out of their mouth and devours their enemies. And if anyone will hurt them, so it is right for him to be killed.
These have authority to shut up the heaven, that it may not rain in the days of their prophecy. And they have authority over waters to turn them to blood, and to strike the earth with every plague, as often as they desire.
And when they complete their testimony, the beast coming up out of the abyss will make war against them and will overcome them and kill them.
And their bodies will lie in the street of the great city, which spiritually is called Sodom and Egypt, where also our Lord was crucified.
And many of the peoples and tribes and tongues and nations will see their dead bodies three days and a half, and they will not allow their dead bodies to be put in tombs.

And the ones who dwell on the earth will rejoice over them, and will make merry, and will send one another gifts, because these two prophets tormented those living on the earth.

And after three days and a half, a spirit of life from God entered into them, and they stood on their feet. And great fear fell on those seeing them.

And they heard a great voice from Heaven saying to them, Come up here. And they went up to Heaven in a cloud, and their enemies watched them.

And in that hour a great earthquake occurred, and the tenth part of the city fell. And seven thousand names of men were slain in the earthquake. And the rest were frightened and gave glory to the God of Heaven." (Revelation 11:4-13, MKJV)

It appears then that the final prophet that comes in the spirit of Elijah will eventually team up with another prophet in the spirit of Moses. They will preach the final messages of the need for repentance in religious and civil matters, before wars requiring Christ's returns to stop the wars. Jesus Christ will then end the rebellion against God, the destruction, and the madness of humankind living in defiance of God.

Jesus Christ, the greatest Prophet, sent the warning that till His return, there may be no other prophet that deems himself as great or perhaps even greater than Jesus Christ. There can only be preachers, pastors, and evangelists, supported by elders and deacons and deaconesses. Any person trying to be a prophet can only preach what has already been prophesied. There is no new prescription for salvation. There can be no new spiritual Law. The path to salvation has been given and prepared in great detail. We all have Bibles. No new book or form of worship can come as though Jesus Christ's Ministry was incomplete or inadequate.

"And the Spirit and the bride say, Come! And let the one hearing say, Come! And let the one who is thirsty come. And he willing, let him take of the Water of Life freely.
For I testify together to everyone who hears the Words of the prophecy of this Book: If anyone adds to these things, God will add on him the plagues that have been written in this Book.
And if anyone takes away from the Words of the Book of this prophecy, God will take away his part out of the Book of Life, and out of the holy city, and from the things which have been written in this Book."
(Revelation 22:17-19, MKJV)

Neither of these prophets or witnesses has arrived since the First Advent of Christ. We know the indications, and what we can expect. They will still appear on the scene at a future time. The rest of the alleged great prophets have died and has to be rejected. They were not prophets in the spirit of Moses or Elijah because Christ did not return in their lifetime. Some may be seen as evangelists or pastors. Some may have had the ability to explain the written prophecies. But if they deviate from the previously established scriptures, they cannot be a great prophet. We have a true witness in the Bible. All people can acquire a Bible and study it. The road to salvation has been established. We cannot deviate from it.

We only regard the Greatest Prophet of all time: Jesus the Christ, our Savior, our High Priest!

Chapter 10

The Final Revelation

We need to consider wisdom from the final revelation granted to the beloved apostle of Jesus Christ. John, the apostle, may have been the longest living disciple and full apostle that Jesus Christ had personal dealings with during His first advent. He was considered the apostle of love. Jesus really loved him, perhaps more than the others. John was selected by Jesus when He started His ministry and was designated as one of the twelve that will one day rule with Christ over the twelve tribes of Israel in the seventh millennium. Notice the answer to the apostle Peter:

"Then answering Peter said to Him, Behold, we have forsaken all and have followed You. Therefore what shall we have?
And Jesus said to them, Truly I say to you that you who have followed Me, in the regeneration, when the Son of Man shall sit in the throne of His glory, you also shall sit on twelve thrones, judging the twelve tribes of Israel."
(Mathew 19:27-28, MKJV)

The twelve apostles were with Jesus Christ constantly for over three years. They heard Him explain the scriptures. Previously they learned from teachers in the Jewish synagogues and even the temple in Jerusalem.

They also were willing to risk the scorn of the community. They knew enough and proved their loyalty and willingness to obey and follow in the face of danger. They were tested and proven. In the resurrection, they will have special rewards and power to bring on the vision of a New Jerusalem under Jesus Christ.

One of them was the apostle John. Jesus had a special love for John and would lay a special responsibility on him.

"Then Peter, turning around, saw the disciple whom
Jesus loved following (the one who also leaned on His
breast at supper, and said, Lord, who is he who betrays
You?)
Seeing him, Peter said to Jesus, Lord, and what of this
one?
Jesus said to him, If I desire that he remain until I come,
what is that to you? You follow Me.
Then this saying went abroad among the brothers, that
that disciple should not die. Yet Jesus did not say to him,
He shall not die, but, If I desire that he remain until I
come, what is that to you?"
(John 21:20-23, MKJV)

It tuned out that Jesus would return to John in his lifetime in the spirit through a special and final prophecy.

John was taken captive by the Romans, just like some of the other apostles. However, his life was spared to bring the final to prophecy to Christians. Notice the order of an authority. Notice the chain of command:

"A Revelation of Jesus Christ, which God gave to Him to declare to His servants things which must shortly come to pass. And He signified it by sending His angel to His servant John,"
(John 1:1, MKJV)

The revelation comes from God through Jesus Christ, who gave it to the angel to give it to John. Any prophecy to humanity would be to the followers of Christ. It would not deny Christ His divinity. It would not belittle Jesus in any way. All true prophecy would acknowledge the status and position of Jesus the Christ.

Would Christ pass on any prophecy that denies that He is at the right hand of the Father? Would Christ pass on any prophecy that would belittle Jesus Christ? Would God the Father give any prophecy that would belittle the followers of Christ? Obviously not!

We can look at this last prophecy with awe and wonder. It is written in a way that would require the reader to have much prior knowledge. Hence most people will be at a loss trying to understand the prophecy. This prophecy would generally be misunderstood.

We will now endeavor to investigate this last prophesy and will provide an overview to assist the reader in marveling at this work of genius.

The Seven Churches

The first section contains seven messages to seven churches.

"John to the seven churches which are in Asia. Grace to you and peace from Him who is and who was and who is coming; and from the seven spirits which are before His throne;"
(Revelation 1:4, MKJV)

These seven churches happened to have been on a mail route of the typical Roman path. The horses would pull the cart from Rome and do a round route coming back to Rome, dropping off and picking up mail.

What are we to make of this?

Firstly, there were indeed seven churches on this route. These messages may have applied in that day to those churches.

However, there clearly would have been more churches. So there is a bigger message that we should see in this section. These messages show various problems that can arise in churches as they grow. They are warning signs to watch out for. It shows ways in which the congregations can go wrong. These messages are for all churches, that may experience successes but also problems that may come following these successes.

Page | 119

A single church may go through phases as it develops. These messages may be applied to a single church as it grows through lifetimes. As a single church grows, it may experience a success, but if the pastor is not careful, a certain problem may arise from the success. The church may disintegrate if the particular problem is not resolved. If they overcome, a further growth stage may be experienced.

Also, a single person in a church may experience phases of spiritual growth, only to be curtailed by a new problem developing in the believer. Such a person must recognize the problem and overcome if the person is going to keep the faith. If not, the believer may drift away and eventually lose faith.

Then it was also suggested that this would be a general phenomenon in the history of the Christian faith as it spread over the world. We have even seen churches of God trying to identify with a particular suggested phase.

All of the above may be true in one way or another. This prophecy was brilliantly written to assist all churches and believers in their growth.

The Seven Seals

After describing the throne of Almighty God the Father in chapter 4, a further discussion follows of the status of Jesus Christ, the greatest prophet that walked the earth.

From the throne of God, a book with further future events was available from God, but nobody was found worthy of breaking open the seals of this book. This was the book of Revelation. It shows that a suitable intermediary between God and humankind was required to open up a future of building a relationship with humanity.

Firstly the section on the churches shows the mercy of God on the followers of Christ. They would generally be spared future calamity. Now follows the problems that humanity, in general, will face due to ignoring the Messiah.

This was made possible, for God is fair and righteous, and would first allow grace for the Church to evangelize, convert, and call humanity to repentance. But most of humanity would resist, and then face the calamity that will befall people and nations who would not listen, convert, and repent.

Firstly notice how the One worthy of opening the sequence of events is presented:

"And I wept very much, because no one was found worthy to open and to read the book, nor to look at it. And one of the elders said to me, Do not weep. Behold, the Lion of the tribe of Judah, the Root of David, has prevailed to open the book and to loose the seven seals of it.
And I looked, and lo, in the midst of the throne and of the four living creatures, amidst the elders, a Lamb stood, as if it had been slain, having seven horns and seven eyes, which are the seven Spirits of God sent forth into all the earth.
And He came and took the book out of the right hand of Him sitting on the throne."
(Revelation 5:4-7, MKJV)

We must understand the symbolism used. The seven horns, eyes and spirits show how Christ works for the Gospel to be preached in the world, through the Churches over two thousand years.

From chapter 6, we see the sequence of events that played out time and again throughout history.

Firstly a seemingly religious rider on a white horse went out, seemingly to perform a religious work, but consider the way in which it was done. The bow with arrows indicates military conquest. It also shows the rider with the crown, indicating the involvement of earthly kings. But the results are disastrous. What followed were wars, and then economic collapse, and hunger and disease, and eventual death. Such were the results of false religious fervor, causing fighting. All the time, the true peaceful workers of the true Messiah had their evangelism oppressed, and they were persecuted throughout these events.

In Chapter 7, we see the true followers that go forth evangelizing and spreading peaceful ways. They were persecuted by leaders desperate to isolate them. They are noted and will receive rewards in the resurrection.

In Chapter 8, we see how a meteor causes destruction on the earth, wiping out much of unrepentant humanity. This section was unbelievable at first. It did not make sense. However, recently the Hubble telescope placed in the second heaven by NASA, captured how the Shumaker-Levi meteor was pulled apart by the gravity of the planet Jupiter. Sections and boulders the size of small mountains crashed into Jupiter over a period of several hours. As the planet rotated, these sections or boulders would crash one after another all over the planet.

The same will happen on the earth. First smaller rocks and debris will smash into the earth. Later larger rocks will look like burning mountains as they burn through the atmosphere. The first big one will fall into the sea, causing a huge tsunami. Ships will flip over and sink. Others trapped in harbors will be smashed. Later further rocks will explode as they burn and spill unusual matter onto farms and rivers, boosting poisonous algae bloom and red tide to make the water deadly. Dust from this event floats up into the atmosphere and blacks out the sun and moon. This is a real future event. It is a classic semi life extinction event. The earth suffered these before. It will happen again. But God has promised protection for his saints, who truly worship and obey Him.

However, this event will place serious stress on some nations. This leads to the terrible fighting for, and control over, other nations for many months. We see that in chapter 9.

It is clear that the quest is for food. There is no interest in hurting farms or buildings. We see images that look like helicopters with tails, and a noise that sounds like many wings. Chemical warfare will incapacitate the population while others strip the farmlands.

In chapter 10, we see that a further message describes more unfolding events. The message was sweet like honey, but when eaten, it would be bitter in the stomach. This is the case when Messiah returns. Things will not be as expected. The further message is to be withheld till later.

Chapter 11 deals more with the experience of the saints in the Churches of God, and the confrontation between God's truth on the one hand, and deceived and deceiving people on the other hand. It all leads to the return of the Messiah.

Chapter 12 deals with an overview of major events for the Church. Initially, Israel was seen as the Church during the Exodus. Later Israel in and around Jerusalem was considered the Church of God, bearing the first advent of the Messiah. The scenery echoes the events around the ministry and crucifixion of Jesus Christ. It also shows the ongoing work and events of the Church that continued afterward.

From chapter 13, we see successions of world-influencing kingdoms coming over the earth, and in particular, having influence over Jerusalem, the city of God. This parallels the imagery found in the prophecies of Daniel.

From chapter 14, we see how God would be displeased that humankind would not turn to Him and His son to receive His mercies and blessings. The situation on the earth would become progressively worse and worse. There is the desperate plea from evangelists for conversion and repentance, but wrong ideas would be causing nations to disintegrate and fail. In the end, many turn to God with real repentance and honest worship, and Jesus and His saints will overcome the evil of the fallen angels and their arch deceiver. This story is still unfolding and will lead to the return of the Messiah.

This prophecy came from God the Father, through His Son, our Messiah, who was the greatest prophet that walked the earth. His sacrifice proved everything to God the Father as well to mankind. Salvation is now at hand. The story can unfold until the return of Christ. Mankind can be saved from self-destruction. The curse that came with Adam and Eve's disobedience and rebellion can be lifted. God will not leave us to die. Our story can continue forever.

Such is the message of the greatest prophet of all time.

Then finally we are warned not to add nor subtract from the prophecy that came through Jesus Christ:

"For I testify together to everyone who hears the Words of the prophecy of this Book: If anyone adds to these things, God will add on him the plagues that have been written in this Book.
And if anyone takes away from the Words of the Book of this prophecy, God will take away his part out of the Book of Life, and out of the holy city, and from the things which have been written in this Book."
(Revelation 22:18 – 19, MKJV)

The testimony to humanity is complete. God has spoken through His prophets. It culminated with the greatest prophet, Jesus Christ, the Son of God, in person. No further book was added or should be added. The knowledge for salvation is complete. It is up to humanity to take the body of scriptures and learn from it. Once understood, proven, and believed, humanity has the knowledge to reach out to God and eternal life. There is no need for another great prophet, only in the end, in preparation for His Second Advent.

More eBooks available from Pieter C Voges

Harmonizing the Creation Week and Science

Life after Death

Nations of the Last Days

The Flood – can be believe it?

Understanding the Godhead

The Sign of Jonah – Expanded

Fulfillment of the Sin Sacrifice

The Creator's Time Matrix

The Sin Sacrifice

The Greatest Prophet

The Lord of the Sabbath

Fulfillment of the Holy Days and New Moon Sacrifices

About the author

Pieter C Voges grew up in Pretoria, South Africa, and graduated from Langenhoven High School. After studying at Pretoria Technicon and Pretoria University, a career at IBM followed.

Attending various Christian churches led to appointment as a Pastor and Evangelist. Eventually several books were written, and recently converted to eBooks. More is in production.